The "Reason Why" Series

INSECTS AND PLANTS

Irving and Ruth Adler

The John Day Company
New York

An Intext Publisher

THE "REASON WHY" BOOKS

AIR
ATOMIC ENERGY
ATOMS AND MOLECULES
THE CALENDAR
COAL
COMMUNICATION
DIRECTIONS AND ANGLES
ENERGY
THE EARTH'S CRUST
EVOLUTION
FIBERS
HEAT AND ITS USES
HOUSES: FROM CAVES TO SKYSCRAPERS
INSECTS AND PLANTS
INTEGERS: POSITIVE AND NEGATIVE
IRRIGATION: CHANGING DESERTS TO GARDENS
LANGUAGE AND MAN
LEARNING ABOUT STEEL: THROUGH THE STORY OF A NAIL
MACHINES
MAGNETS
NUMBERS OLD AND NEW
NUMERALS: NEW DRESSES FOR OLD NUMBERS
OCEANS
RIVERS
SETS
SHADOWS
STORMS
TASTE, TOUCH AND SMELL
THINGS THAT SPIN: FROM TOPS TO ATOMS
TREE PRODUCTS
WHY? A BOOK OF REASONS
WHY AND HOW? A SECOND BOOK OF REASONS
YOUR EARS
YOUR EYES

Fourth Impression, 1973

© 1962 by Irving and Ruth Adler

All rights reserved. This book, or parts thereof, must not be reproduced in any form without permission. Published by The John Day Company, 257 Park Avenue South, New York, N.Y., and simultaneously in Canada by Longman Canada Limited, Toronto.

Library of Congress Catalogue Card Number: 62-19714
ISBN: 0-381-99966-1 GB

MANUFACTURED IN THE UNITED STATES OF AMERICA

Contents

Insects and Plants	4
Trillions of Insects	6
An Insect's Body	6
Getting Too Big for Its Skin	8
How to Raise Your Own Butterflies	8
Insects That Eat Plants	12
Plants That Eat Insects	14
Insects That Keep "Cows"	16
How a Flower Makes Its Seed	18
Insects That Pollinate Flowers	20
A Flower-Insect Team: The Yucca and the Pronuba Moth	24
Another Team: The Fig and the Fig Wasp	26
Insects That Pay Rent	28
An Air-Conditioned House	29
How Plants Protect Insects	30
Insects That Harm Us	32
A Beetle That Changed Its Diet	34
The Root Louse Crosses the Ocean	34
Some Imported Insect Pests	36
An Australian Friend in a Time of Need	38
An All-American Pest	39
Getting Rid of Insect Pests	40
Plagues	42
Live Weed Killers	42
Honey, Wax, and Ink	44
Insects for Varnish and Dye	46
A Cradle of Silk	47
Word List	48

Insects and Plants

This is a book about insects and plants.

It tells about some of the things that insects do *to* plants. It also tells about some of the things that insects do *for* plants. It also tells about some of the things that plants do *to* insects and *for* insects. It shows how insects and plants are related to each other.

You will find out about insects that pay rent to plants and about insects that go rent-free. You will also find out about insects that live in air-conditioned houses.

You will find out about insects that like nice smells and bright colors. You will learn, too, about insects that like to eat

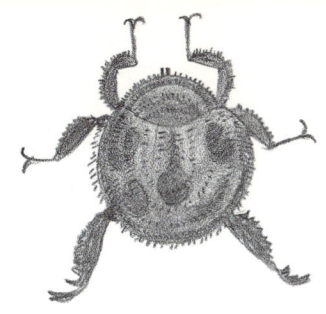 

sweets and that keep "cows" that give them "milk."

You will find out about insects and plants that cannot live without each other. You will learn about an insect that goes on a hunger strike.

You will find out about insects that people *raise* because they eat plants. And you will find out about insects that people *kill* because they eat plants. You will also learn about plants that eat insects.

You will find out about insects that sew and spin and weave and bore.

And you will learn about useful things that people make from some insects and plants that work together.

Trillions of Insects

There are about a million different kinds of animals. There are elephants and mice, cats and dogs, crabs and earthworms, snakes and fish, flies and ladybugs, and monkeys and people. Most of the different kinds of animals are insects. If one animal of each kind marched past you in a parade, out of every hundred animals, 75 of them would be insects!

Insects live all over the world. Most insects live in the warm places on the earth where most of the other animals also live. Most insects get their food by eating plants.

Because there are so many insects, it is important for people to find out all they can about them. Then they can learn how to use insects to help them. They can also learn how to keep insects from harming them.

An Insect's Body

An insect has a body with a hard outside cover. The cover protects the soft parts inside. The body has three main parts.

The front part of the body is the head. On the head are a pair of eyes, a pair of hairy feelers called *antennae* (an-TEN-ee), and mouth parts. Some insects have mouth parts that can chew. Other insects have mouth parts that can suck.

The next part of the body is called the *thorax* (THORE-ax). Three pairs of legs are attached to the thorax. The legs have joints, so they bend easily. Many insects have wings. The wings are attached to the thorax, too.

The back part of an insect's body is the *abdomen* (ab-DOE-men). The abdomen looks something like a worm. Insects that sting have their stinging parts on the abdomen. The egg-laying parts of insects are on the abdomen, too.

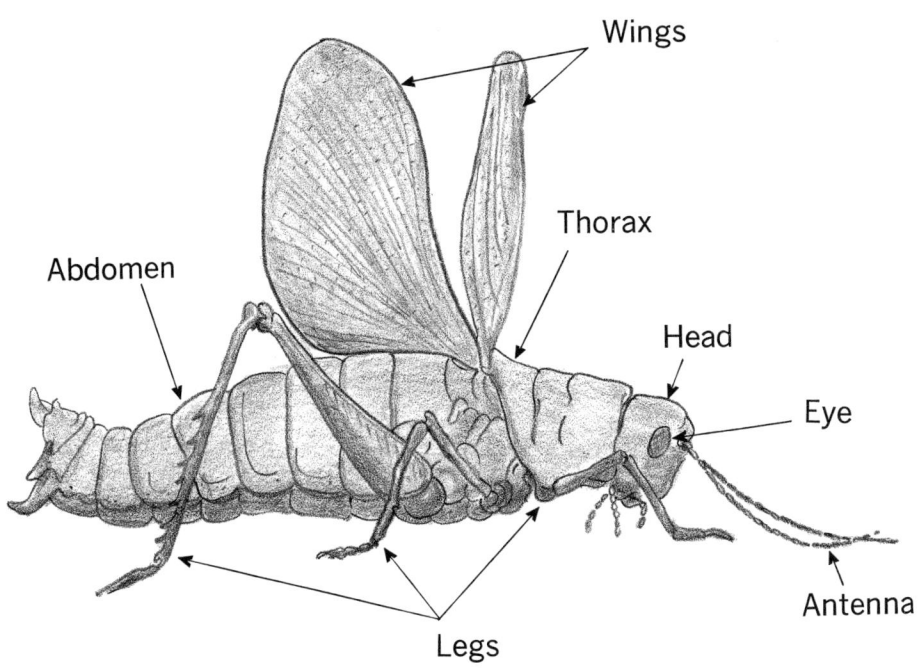

An insect's body

Getting Too Big for Its Skin

All insects hatch out of eggs.

A newly hatched baby *grasshopper* looks a lot like a grown-up grasshopper. But it is small and has no wings. As it grows, it gets too big for its skin. Then the skin splits and the baby grasshopper walks out of it and leaves the skin behind in the grass. You can find empty grasshopper skins in hayfields. The grasshopper keeps on growing and splitting its skin. Its wings develop. Finally it is full-grown.

Other insects change a few times before they become full-grown or *adult* (a-DULT). This is true of butterflies, for example. Monarch butterflies are easy to raise. So you can watch all these changes when you raise your own Monarch butterflies.

How to Raise Your Own Butterflies

You begin to see the *Monarch* butterfly in fields and gardens in the northern part of the United States in May and June. The butterfly has brown wings with black lines on them, and rows of white dots near the edges.

The female Monarch butterfly always lays its eggs on the milkweed plant. The milkweed is the only food the newly hatched babies will eat. You can find Monarch eggs on the underneath side of young leaves. They are white and about the size of a pinhead. The picture shows you what they look like.

Pick the milkweed leaves with the eggs on them, and put them into a big glass jar. Make air holes in the cover of the jar.

After a few days the eggs will hatch. The newly hatched Monarch baby does not look at all like an adult insect. It is a tiny caterpillar with yellow, black and white stripes. It is called the *larva* of the insect. The caterpillar begins to eat the leaves of the milkweed. It keeps eating all the time. It grows very fast. It splits its skin a few times, the way the baby grasshopper does. It grows until it is about two inches long. This takes about two weeks. You will want to keep fresh milkweed leaves in the jar while the caterpillar is growing. You will also want to clean out caterpillar droppings.

Egg
(drawn many times larger)

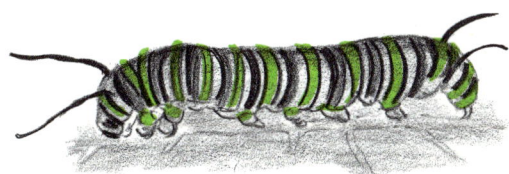
Caterpillar

Then the caterpillar stops eating. It crawls to the top of the jar, where it weaves a little mat of silk. The back part of the caterpillar hooks into the silk mat. The caterpillar hangs with its head down. Then the caterpillar begins to wiggle and twist. It wiggles and twists so hard that its skin splits, starting at its head. It pulls together and becomes short and thick. It hasn't the yellow, black and white stripes of the caterpillar any more. In fact it isn't a caterpillar any more. The caterpillar has changed into a *pupa* (PEW-pa) or chrysalis (KRISS-a-lis). The pupa looks like a pea-green jewel with golden nails.

The pupa hangs from its silk mat without moving for about 10 days. You must be careful not to shove or bang the jar at this time. If you look at the pupa every day, you will notice that it is changing. First the pupa begins to turn gray. Then it becomes so clear that you can see inside it. You can see a Monarch butterfly folded up inside.

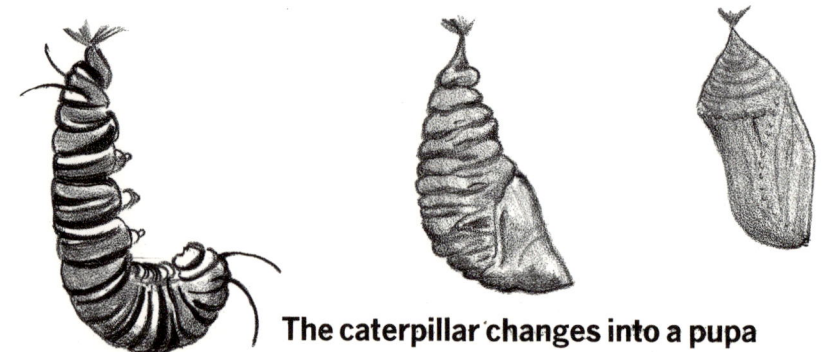

The caterpillar changes into a pupa

The butterfly is the adult insect.

Now the butterfly is ready to hatch. If you are lucky, you will be watching when the pupa splits and the butterfly comes out. The newly hatched butterfly hangs by its legs, with its head down. Its abdomen is very fat. Its wings are very small. You can see something like a heartbeat moving in the abdomen. With each beat, the abdomen gets smaller and the wings get bigger. With each beat, blood is pumped from the abdomen into the wings.

When the wings are full of blood, the butterfly begins to walk around. You can hold it in your hand for a long time and it will not fly away. It cannot fly, because its wings are still wet. After a few hours, when its wings are dry, it will fly away.

After the male and female butterflies mate, the female is ready to lay eggs. She looks for a milkweed plant. Then you can start raising butterflies again.

The newly hatched butterfly

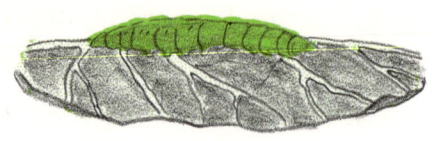 

Cabbage worm   **Cabbage butterfly**

Insects That Eat Plants

The *cabbage butterfly* lays its eggs on the leaves of plants in the cabbage family. It lays its eggs on nasturtiums, too. These plants are the only food that its larva, the cabbage worm, will eat. If cabbage worms are moved to other kinds of plants, they will go on a hunger strike and die. But they can be fooled into eating other plants. If the sap of cabbages or nasturtiums is rubbed on the leaves of other plants, the cabbage worms will begin to eat these plants, too.

Many plant-eating insects, like cabbage worms, are *free feeders*. Free feeders can move around easily over the plant on which they are feeding.

Some plant-eating insects are trapped on the plants on which they feed. *Scale insects* and *gall insects* are trapped in this way.

Male adult scale insects have no mouth parts. So they cannot eat. The female adults attach themselves by their mouth parts to the plants on which they feed. Their bodies make a scaly stuff. The scale of some insects is waxy. The scale of other insects is cottony. The scale covers the feeding insects and hides them. It looks like part of the plant on which the insects are feeding.

The female gall insect lays her egg in a hole she makes in a leaf or twig. When the egg hatches into a larva, the leaf or twig around the larva begins to grow in a strange way. It grows into a *gall*, which looks something like a round nut. As the larva grows, the gall grows too. So the larva always has plenty of food.

Most plants have many insects that feed on them. About 1,000 different kinds of insects feed on oak trees. Some of them are gall insects. The oak "apple" is made by a gall. There are insects that even feed on poison ivy.

Oak "apples"

Plants That Eat Insects

Plants get water and chemicals from the soil through their roots. The water and chemicals help make the plants grow. Some plants do not have big roots. They grow in soil that does not have all the chemicals they need. These plants get the chemicals from insects that they catch and eat.

The *pitcher plant* grows in wet places in the woods. Its leaves are reddish-green. They are shaped like pitchers. Insects that crawl into the open pitcher cannot get out again. There are rows of hairs on the inside, near the open end of the pitcher. The hairs all face down. They work like a barbed-wire fence, and keep the insects inside. The insects fall to the bottom of the pitcher and die. Chemicals in the pitcher plant change the insects into food to make the plant grow.

The *sundew* is another plant that catches and eats insects. Its leaves look like fuzzy caterpillars at the end of

Pitcher plant

long thin stems. A sticky sap comes out of the fuzzy hairs on the leaves. Insects get caught in the sticky sap. When an insect is caught, the hairs bend over and hold the insect tightly, so that it cannot get away. Chemicals in the sticky sap change the insects into food for the sundew.

The *Venus's flytrap* catches insects with the speed of a mousetrap. At the end of each wide leaf is a trap that looks like a round box, with a hinge down the middle. The edges of the trap end in a row of stiff, pointed hairs. There are tiny hairs on the inside of the trap, too. Insects go inside the trap because of a sweet sap they find there. When an insect steps on the tiny hairs, the two parts of the trap close very quickly. The stiff, pointed hairs come together the way your fingers do when you clasp your hands. The insect is trapped and cannot get out. Chemicals inside the trap change the insect into other chemicals that the plant can use as food.

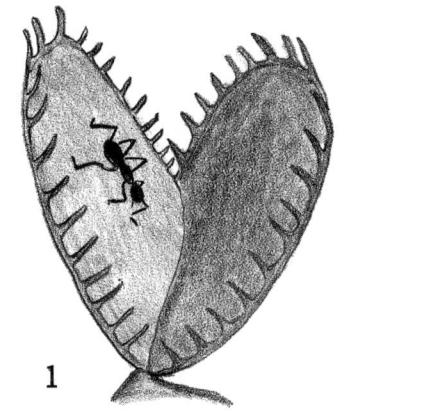
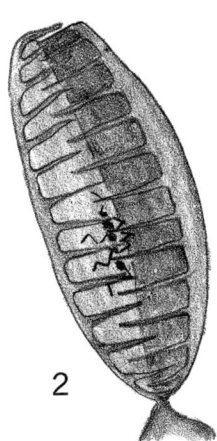
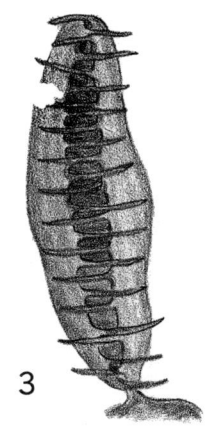

A Venus's flytrap catches an insect

An ant and its "cow"

Insects That Keep "Cows"

People who park their cars on tree-lined streets find it hard to keep their cars clean and shiny. The cars are soon covered with tiny drops of a sticky stuff. This stuff is *honeydew*. It is made by a small insect called an *aphid* (AFF-id). The aphid is a sucking insect. It has mouth parts that look like a drinking straw. It sucks the sap from the leaves of the trees. The sap is changed inside the aphid's body into sweet honeydew. There are two little openings at the back end of the aphid from which the honeydew flows. Ants come to drink the honeydew. If there aren't enough ants to gather all the honeydew, the sticky drops fall to the ground.

There are tree ants in India that take care of aphids the way a farmer cares for his cows. They sew together the leaves of trees to make a shed in which they keep the aphids. The ants use a live needle that makes its own thread. The needle is one of their own larvae. The thread is silk that is spun by the larvae. The picture shows how some of the ants pull the edges of two leaves together. Other ants hold the larvae in their jaws. They push the larvae back and forth between the edges of the leaves. As they do this, the larvae spin a sticky silk thread. The thread sticks to the edges of the leaves. It sews the leaves together to make a dry shed for the ant "cows."

There are aphids that feed on the roots of corn plants. In many places, it gets too cold in the wintertime for the aphids to stay alive. These aphids are cared for by ants who gather their honeydew. The ants carry the aphids to places deeper in the ground where it is not as cold. Then the aphids do not die. In the springtime, the ants carry the aphids back to the corn plant.

Ants "sewing" a leaf shed

How a Flower Makes Its Seed

Many plants have flowers that make their seeds. The flowers have male parts and female parts. The male parts make a fine yellow powder called *pollen*. To make a seed, pollen must be brought from a male part to a female part. This is called *pollination* (poll-in-AY-shun). For some plants the work of pollination is done by insects.

The male part of a flower is called the *stamen* (STAY-men). The *anther* (AN-ther) is a little knob at the end of the stamen. Pollen is made in the anther.

The female part of a flower is called the *pistil* (PIS-till). The bottom part of the pistil is shaped like a large,

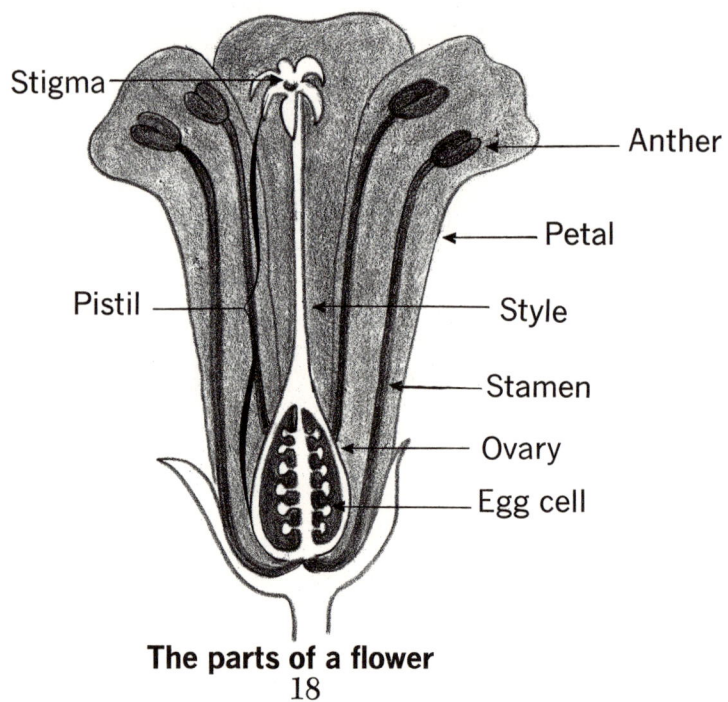

The parts of a flower

round bead. This part is called the *ovary* (O-va-ree). There are eggs cells in the ovary. The end of the pistil is called the *stigma* (STIG-ma). The stigma is attached to the ovary by a thin tube called the *style*.

Insects that pollinate flowers carry the pollen from the anther of one flower to the stigma of another flower. The stigma is usually sticky, so the pollen is held there. Then the pollen grain grows a long thin tube. The tube goes down into the ovary. Some of the stuff inside the pollen goes down the tube into the ovary. It comes together with an egg cell in the ovary. The egg has been fertilized (FUR-till-ized). The fertilized egg becomes a flower seed.

The pistil is in the center of the flower. The stamens are around the pistil. The *petals* are around the pistil and the stamens. The petals often have bright colors. The bright colors help bring insects to the flowers.

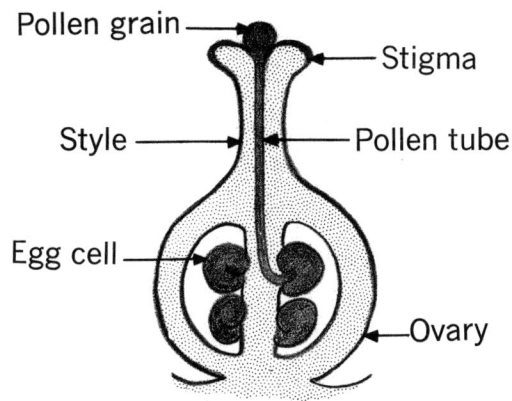

An egg cell is fertilized

A bee gathering pollen and nectar

Insects That Pollinate Flowers

Flowers of different plants have different shapes, colors and odors. Some flowers have sweet smells. Some flowers smell like animal dung. Some flowers make *nectar* (NECK-tar). Nectar is a sweet liquid that insects gather as food. Insects also gather pollen as food. The shapes, colors and smells of flowers bring insects to them.

When an insect visits a flower to get food, some pollen sticks to the insect's body. Then, when the insect flies on to another flower of the same kind, it carries pollen to it. Bees, butterflies, wasps, moths, beetles and flies all carry pollen from one flower to another.

Flowers that are pollinated by bees are usually yellow and blue. This is because bees cannot see all colors. They see mostly yellow and blue. Bee flowers have sweet smells. Bees will not visit flowers with bad smells. Bees fly only during the daytime. So many bee flowers are open during the daytime and closed at night. The petals of some bee flowers come together to make a thin tube. The nectar is at the bottom of the tube. The long thin tongue of the bee can gather the nectar of these flowers. Some orchids are bee flowers. Peas, violets and clover are bee flowers, too.

The nectar of butterfly and moth flowers is at the bottom of a long tube, too. Almost all butterflies and moths have very long tongues. There is a moth with a tongue 10 inches long. Moths usually fly in the evening and at night. So moth flowers do not have bright colors. Many moth flowers are closed during the daytime and open up in the evening. Morning-glory, tobacco, yucca and evening primroses are moth flowers. Butterflies feed during the daytime. Red and orange are colors that some butter-

These lilies are butterfly flowers

flies can see. For this reason, many butterfly flowers are red and orange. Carnations and many lilies are butterfly flowers.

Some fly flowers have very bad smells. Flies with short tongues get most of their food from dung or rotting plants and animals. So these flies visit plants that smell like the food they are used to.

Beetles visit flowers because of their smell. Beetle flowers usually have big blossoms that grow alone. Wild roses, pond lilies and magnolias are beetle flowers. Beetles are not happy just to gather nectar from flowers. They also eat the petals.

Some insects are trapped for days by the flowers they visit. Hairs inside the flower keep the insect from escaping. While the insect is inside the flower, the pollen ripens on the stamens. The trapped insect gets covered

The pond lily is a beetle flower

A fly caught in a milkweed flower

with pollen. After a few days, the hairs drop off and the insect is able to leave the flower. It flies to another flower just like the one in which it was trapped. Here it is trapped again for a few days. So the pollen the insect carries has plenty of time to rub off. Some of the pollen rubs off on the stigma and pollination takes place.

The milkweed plant is unkind to some insects that visit it. There are deep cracks in the anthers where the pollen is formed. Insects slip when they step on the flower to gather nectar. They slip into the deep cracks, where their legs get caught. Pollen sticks to their legs. The insects try hard to get free. Some insects never free themselves. Others lose a leg in the struggle. The insects that get free then fly on to another milkweed blossom, where the same thing happens. While they are fighting to free themselves again, they leave some pollen on the flower's stigma.

A Flower-Insect Team: The Yucca and the Pronuba Moth

The *yucca* flower and the *Pronuba* (pron-YOU-ba) moth cannot live without each other. They work together as a team.

The flowers of yucca plants open up and the Pronuba moth becomes an adult at exactly the same time. They are ready for mating at exactly the same time. Each one needs the other to help it mate.

The Pronuba moths come to the yucca flower because of its sweet smell. Male and female moths fly around inside the blossom and mate there. The female Pronuba moth has special mouth parts with which she can scrape. After mating, the female moth scrapes sticky pollen from the anthers of the yucca. She presses the pollen together, and rolls it into a ball. She carries the ball of pollen the way a child carries a balloon tucked under his chin. She carries the ball of pollen to another yucca flower. She makes a hole in the ovary of the second flower, and lays an egg. The egg of the moth is now in the ovary of the flower.

After the moth has laid her egg, she climbs up onto the stigma. She takes part of the ball of pollen that she carries and pushes it into the opening of the stigma. Then she lays another egg in the ovary. After laying the second egg, she pushes some more pollen into the stigma. She lays about five eggs. She pushes pollen into the stigma after each egg is laid. In this way the female moth has laid her eggs and pollinated the yucca flower at the same time.

When the eggs hatch into larvae, seeds have already formed in the ovary of the yucca. The larvae eat some of the seeds. This is how the yucca pays the moth for its help. After a month of eating seeds, the larvae eat their way out of the ovary. They fall to the ground. They grow up to be adult moths. They become adults at exactly the same time that the yucca flowers bloom again.

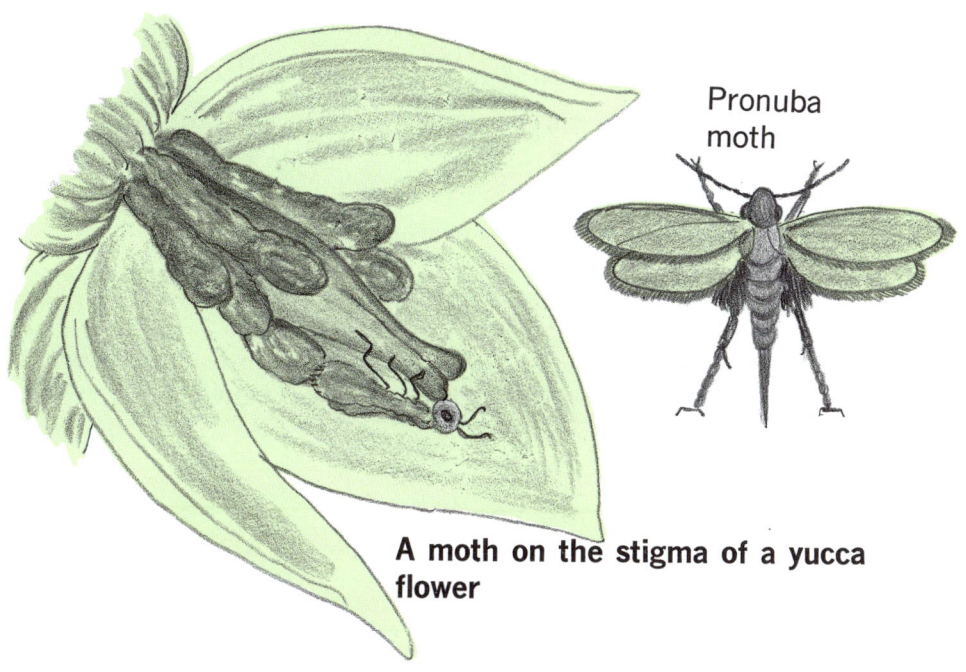

Pronuba moth

A moth on the stigma of a yucca flower

Another Team: The Fig and the Fig Wasp

Sweet figs grow on the *Smyrna fig* trees of Turkey, Italy, and Spain. It is warm and sunny in all these countries. It is also warm and sunny in southern California. So fruitgrowers decided to raise Smyrna figs in southern California.

At first the fig growers were disappointed. The figs that grew on California Smyrna fig trees were small and sour. Fig growers wanted to find out the reason for this. Their search for the answer was like a detective story. The clue to the answer was a tiny little wasp.

The Smyrna fig is a thick, soft shell shaped like a pear. There are hundreds of flowers inside the shell. The flowers are all female. When a flower is fertilized, a seed forms. Each flower makes only one seed. A fig will be

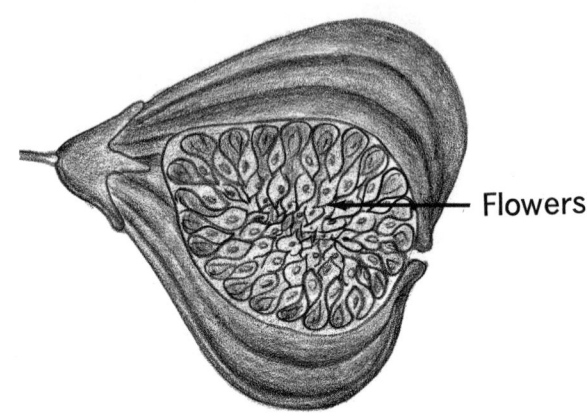

A fig with part of it cut away

very sweet if it has a lot of seeds in it. So a fig will [be] sweet if many of its flowers have been pollina[ted.] is where the mystery begins. The Smyrna fig makes [no] *pollen.* How do its flowers get pollinated?

There is a wild fig called the *caprifig* (CAP-ri-fig). Its figs do not taste good. But its flowers are male flowers, with plenty of pollen. A little wasp lives in the caprifig. It develops inside a wild fig and feeds on it. The male wasp has no wings and never leaves the caprifig. It mates with the female wasp while she is still inside the fig. After mating, the female crawls out of the caprifig. As she does so, she gets covered with pollen.

The female wasp has wings. She flies to another fig to lay her eggs. If she lands on a caprifig, she lays her eggs and new wasps develop. If she lands on a Smyrna fig, she walks around inside the fig looking for a place to lay her eggs. She does not lay her eggs there, because the eggs will not develop inside a Smyrna fig. But something else happens. Pollen from the caprifig rubs off her body onto the female flowers of the Smyrna figs. In this way the flowers are fertilized and seeds develop, making sweet Smyrna figs.

When the fig growers of California found out how Smyrna figs were pollinated, they brought caprifigs and fig wasps to the United States. Now California grows sweet Smyrna figs.

Insects That Pay Rent

There are plants that give insects a place to live. The insects, in turn, pay rent to the plants for their safe homes. They pay the plants by keeping away other insects that might harm the plant. Many ants help trees in this way.

There are long hollow thorns on the *hull-horn acacia* tree that grows in Brazil and Central America. Tiny ants live in these thorns. They get inside by making a hole in the pointed end of the thorn. The hollow inside makes a fine home in which the ants raise their young. They get their food from the tree, too. They suck a sweet sap from the stems of the acacia leaves. The ants keep leaf-eating insects away from the tree. So the ants always have plenty of leaf sap for food. At the same time, the ants protect the acacia tree.

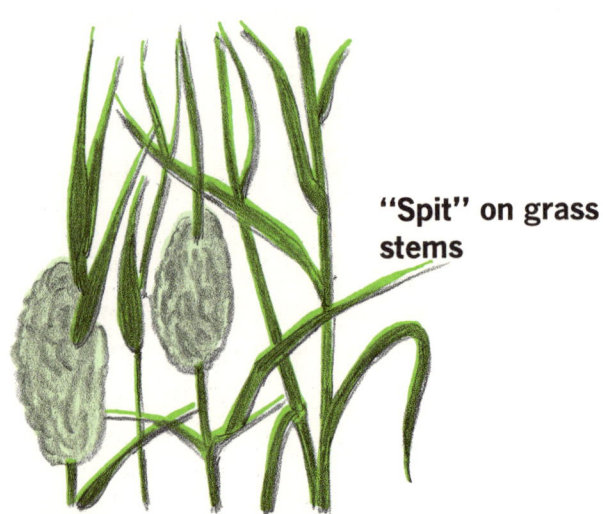

"Spit" on grass stems

An Air-Conditioned House

You can see lumps of "spit" on the stems of grass and weeds in the springtime and summertime. If you take away the spit carefully, you will find out what has made it. You will find a small insect that looks like a tiny frog. It is a young *froghopper*. The froghopper uses sap that it sucks from the plants for making the spit. Its abdomen is built so that it works like a bicycle pump. The froghopper pumps air into the sap. Air bubbles are trapped in the sap. This makes the sap look like spit. The insect stays inside the lump of spit. It is cool and wet inside. The young froghopper is safe from the hot sun in his air-conditioned house.

A froghopper making "spit"

How Plants Protect Insects

The color or shape of an insect is often a matter of life or death. The color and shape of many insects protect them from their most dangerous enemies, birds.

The color or shape of some insects is like the color or shape of the plant on which the insect lives. When the insect is on the plant, the insect is hard to see. Then, its bird enemies do not attack it.

It isn't easy to see a grasshopper in the green grass until the grasshopper begins to hop around.

The *walking-stick* insect gets its name because it looks like a twig. It cannot be seen easily among dead twigs.

There is a caterpillar that looks like a twig, too. It looks like the twig of the birch tree. This caterpillar makes its home on the birch tree where it is hard to see.

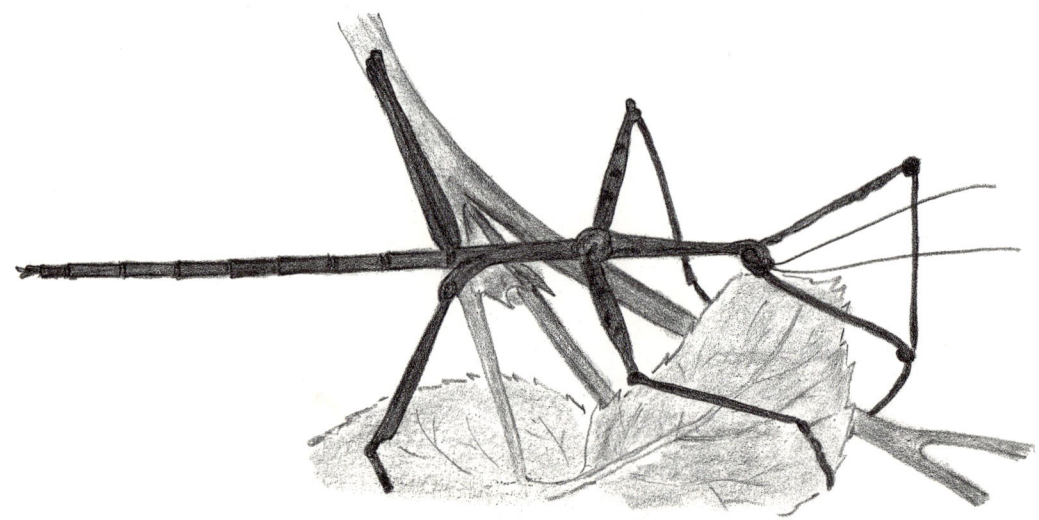

A walking-stick insect

The thorax of the *thorn treehopper* is pointed. It looks like a big thorn. So the thorn treehopper cannot be seen when it rests on thorn trees.

Anglewing butterflies have wings that look torn and ragged. The underneath side of the anglewing is brownish-gray. When the anglewing is at rest in the woods, its ragged brownish-gray wings look just like dead leaves.

There are some insects that are protected by colors that make them easy to see. The *cinnabar-moth* (SIN-a-bar) caterpillar is an example. The caterpillar has bright yellow and black stripes. Many of these caterpillars feed together on ragwort, a plant with small leaves. So the caterpillar is not hidden by the plant on which it feeds. It can be seen very easily from quite far away. *Because* it can be seen easily, its color protects it from its bird enemies. The caterpillar has a bad taste. Birds do not like to eat it. So, when birds see the caterpillars feeding together, they stay away.

The thornhopper looks like a thorn

Insects That Harm Us

Some insects are harmful because they damage or even wipe out plants that people use. Then there is less food for animals that people raise. Then there is also less food for people. And there are less cotton, wood, tobacco and other things that people get from plants.

Only a few of the many kinds of insects are harmful. These insects weren't always harmful. One way insects become harmful is by being moved from a place where they have always lived to a place where they have never lived.

Insects that have been in a place for a long, long time have made enemies. Their enemies may be diseases that kill them. Their enemies may be birds or other insects that eat them. Their enemies kill many of them. So, when insects have been in a place for a long, long time, there are usually not so many of them that they can do much harm.

When insects are moved to a place where they have never lived before, they may find no enemies there. So the number of insects of that kind gets bigger very fast. The insects may still eat the same kind of plant. But because there are so many insects, they can eat up all the plants.

When insects are moved to another place they may

begin to eat plants that they never ate before. Then the new plants are in danger of being eaten up. In some cases insects become harmful when new plants are brought to the place where the insects live. The insects may take a liking to the new plant. Then the insects will begin to go to new places looking for the new plant. Since the insects have no natural enemies in the new places, they become an insect pest there.

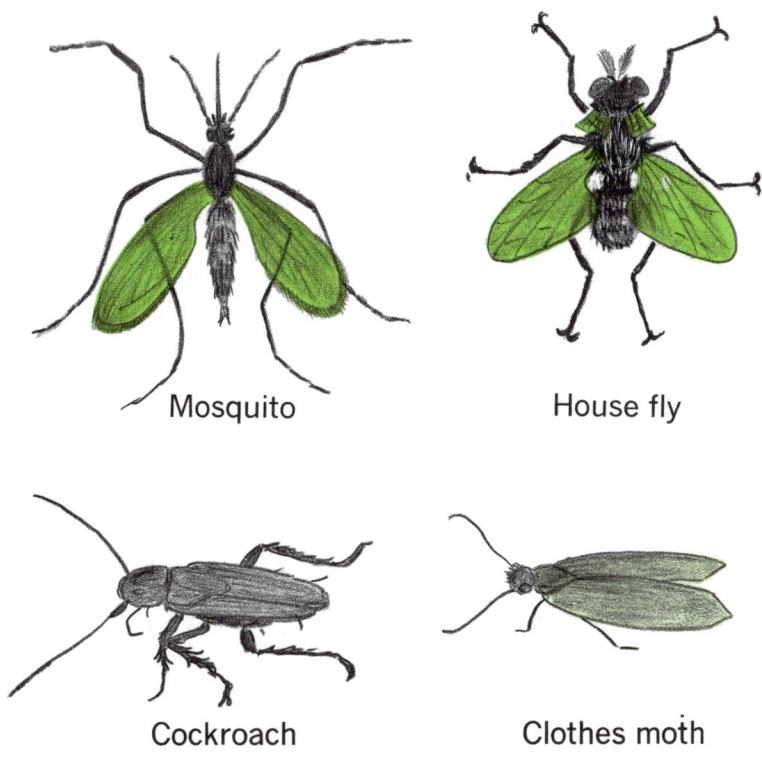

Some insect pests

A potato beetle

A Beetle That Changed Its Diet

The *Colorado potato beetle* wasn't always a potato beetle. At first it lived only in the southwest of the United States on a diet of weeds. When the early American settlers moved west to California they carried potato plants with them. The Colorado beetle liked the taste of potatoes very much. Wherever potatoes were planted, the beetles found their way to them. In this way the beetles spread across the United States. It took them 15 years to eat their way from California to New York.

The Root Louse Crosses the Ocean

For a long time American grape growers tried to grow grapes from vines brought from France. The vines always died. They had been killed by an aphid, the *root louse*, which spent part of its life eating the roots of the grapevine. Grapevines that had always grown in the United States were not damaged by this insect. The roots of American vines were very tough.

About 100 years ago, some American grapevines were brought into France. The root louse came into France on the roots of the vines. In just a few years, it killed almost all the vines in France and in other parts of Europe, too.

Some good came out of this terrible experience. The French grape growers found out how they could grow healthy plants. They attached French vines to the tough roots of the American plant. They did this by *grafting*. The new vines grew grapes with the fine flavor of French grapes. They were not attacked by the root louse because they had the strong roots of American plants.

These new vines were brought back to the United States where they could grow, too. Now American grape growers can grow French grapes in the United States.

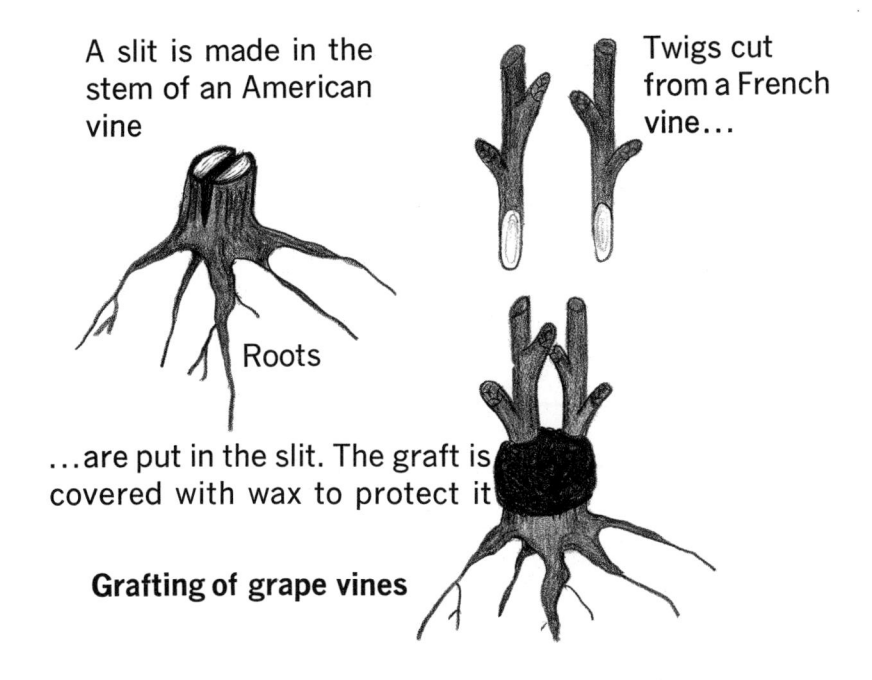

A slit is made in the stem of an American vine

Roots

Twigs cut from a French vine...

...are put in the slit. The graft is covered with wax to protect it

Grafting of grape vines

Some Imported Insect Pests

Most of the insects that have become pests in the United States have been brought in from other countries where they were not harmful. They became pests in the United States because they found no natural enemies to keep them from spreading.

The *gypsy moth* was brought into Massachusetts about 100 years ago by a French scientist who was trying to make silk. Some caterpillars escaped from his laboratory. The caterpillars discovered quickly that they liked eating the leaves of American shade trees. They spread to other states and even to Canada. Many trees were killed. People have learned how to keep the gypsy moth from spreading. They spray trees with poisons. They also inspect plants that are shipped from one state to another to make sure there are no gypsy moths on them.

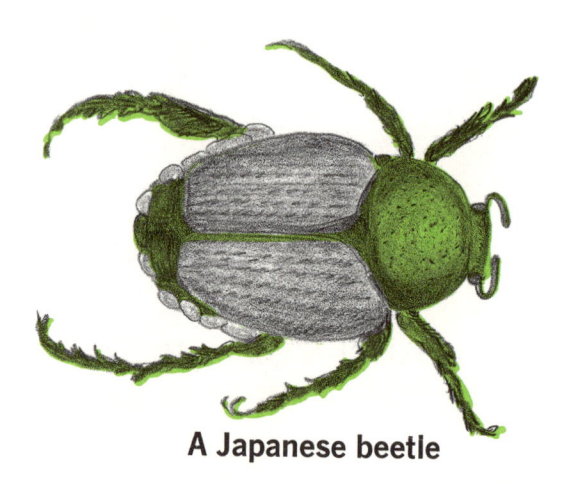

A Japanese beetle

The *Japanese beetle* was first noticed in the United States in 1916. It was living on some fancy Japanese trees in a tree nursery in New Jersey. People didn't know how harmful the beetle could be, so they left it alone. The beetle spread quickly because it found it liked to eat hundreds of other trees and bushes, too. It has been hard to control. It has even been found in airplanes.

The *corn borer* is the larva of a moth. It has always lived in Europe and Asia where there was no corn. It found it liked corn when corn was brought to Europe from America. In fact, it likes corn better than anything else. From the time its eggs hatch in July, the larvae have a nice, comfortable home in the corn plant. They bore their way into tight, dark places inside the plant. They have lots of food all the time. They have a winter home in dead cornstalks. One way to control corn borers is by planting corn at just the right time.

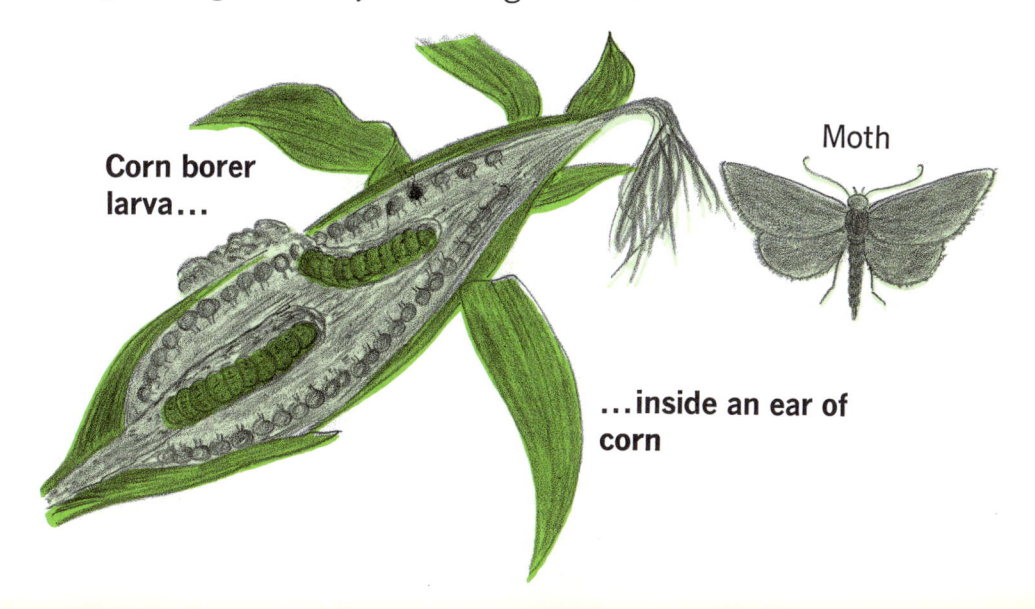

Corn borer larva...

Moth

...inside an ear of corn

An Australian Friend in a Time of Need

The *cottony-cushion scale* is a small scale insect that eats the sap, leaves and twigs of *citrus* (SIT-rus) trees. It was first found in California orange, lemon and grapefruit orchards about 100 years ago. Within 15 years many citrus trees had been killed by the scale and farmers lost their whole crop of citrus fruits.

Some people thought that the scale was brought into California on fruit trees that came from Australia. They thought this because they knew that the cottony-cushion scale had lived in Australia for a long time. They also knew that it was not an insect pest in Australia. So they went to Australia to find out why.

They found their answer in a little reddish-brown lady beetle, the *vedalia beetle*. This beetle and its larvae ate the larvae and eggs of the cottony-cushion scale and *nothing else*.

About 500 vedalia beetles were brought into California from Australia. There was plenty of food for them,

A vedalia beetle

so there were many of them in a short time. In less than two years there were so many vedalia beetles in California that the cottony-cushion scale stopped being a pest.

An All-American Pest

The *boll weevil* is a little black bug with a long snout. It came from Mexico. It likes to eat only the cotton plant. The adult eats the leaves of the cotton plant. With its snout, the female bores holes in the buds of the cotton plant. She lays her eggs inside the buds. Larvae hatch from the eggs. The larvae eat the inside of the bud. Then the bud never grows into a cotton boll. She lays her eggs in the cotton bolls, too. The larvae spoil the cotton inside the boll, so that it cannot be used.

The boll weevil came into the United States through Texas in 1892. It can be found now in all the cotton-growing states in the South. Cotton farmers can keep it under control by using good seed and taking good care of their land.

A boll weevil

Getting Rid of Insect Pests

Insect pests do a lot of harm. They eat crops and hurt trees. They damage houses and clothing. We can never get rid of all insect pests. But we can learn how to control them.

One way to control insect pests is by finding their natural enemies. Chinese citrus-fruit growers controlled insect pests this way for a long time. The citrus trees of China are bothered by a small black fly. Certain ants are the natural enemies of the citrus fly. The fruitgrowers put these ants into their citrus trees. They even make "ant bridges" out of bamboo poles, to make it easier for the ants to go from one tree to another. There are people who make a living raising ants for the fruitgrowers. Germs are sometimes natural enemies of insects. So germs that hurt insects but do not hurt animals or people are sometimes sprayed on plants which insects eat.

Another way to control insect pests is to stop growing plants that insects like and grow instead another plant of the same kind that insects do not like. The *Hessian fly* used to be a pest on American wheat. So scientists looked for a wheat that the Hessian fly would not eat. They found such a wheat plant in southern Europe. They brought this plant to the United States. The European wheat grew well in the United States, because the Hessian fly did not like it.

Another way to control insect pests is to spray poison on the plants on which insects live. This way can be dangerous. It can be dangerous, when poisons are used on food plants. The poisons can hurt people. It can be dangerous, too, because the poisons can kill the natural enemies of the insect pests at the same time. Then, if the insect pests come back again, they spread very quickly. It can be dangerous because the poisons can go into the soil and poison the streams. This happened in Florida when a poison was used to control the sand-fly, an insect pest. Not only were the sand-flies killed, but all of the fish in the area were killed, too.

Another way to control insects is to keep them from spreading from one country to another. This can be done by making sure that all plants that come into a country have no insects on them.

Spraying plants to kill insect pests

USDA photograph

Plagues

It is a bright sunny day. There are fields of grain as far as the eye can see. The wind makes the grain ripple, so that the fields look like a great golden sea.

Suddenly it becomes very dark. The sun is hidden behind a black cloud. But this is not a storm cloud. The cloud moves very quickly, and makes a loud buzzing noise. It is a cloud made up of millions of grasshoppers looking for a new place to live.

After the grasshoppers have passed, the fields are bare. The trees are bare. The grasshoppers have eaten everything.

When this happened a long time ago, it was very terrible. People had no food because the grasshoppers had eaten it all. Thousands of people died. This was what a grasshopper *plague* (PLAYG) did.

Grasshoppers still do a lot of damage. But people usually don't die when grasshoppers eat their crops. People all over the world try to help each other. If people in one part of the world do not have enough food, people in other parts of the world often help them by sending them food.

Live Weed Killers

Weeds are plants that grow where they are not wanted. They grow in gardens and fields crowding out plants that are raised for food.

We usually don't think of the *cactus* plant as a weed. It is a pretty desert plant in the United States. We even keep it as a house plant.

The cactus plant became a weed in Australia. It was brought into Australia by accident in 1787. But the cactus had no natural enemies in Australia. So it spread very quickly. By 1925 millions of acres of land were filled with the weed. Nothing else could grow in them.

Australian scientists came to America to see if they could find the natural enemy of the cactus plant. They brought many different insects back with them. The insects kept the cacti from spreading, but did not wipe them out. Finally, after ten years of searching, the right insect-enemy was found. It was a moth that lived in Argentina. Billions of its eggs were sent to Australia. In seven years all of the cactus plants were wiped out. Then the land could be used again for crops and pasture.

Cactus plants before . . .   . . . and after the moths came.

Dept. of Public Lands, Queensland, Australia

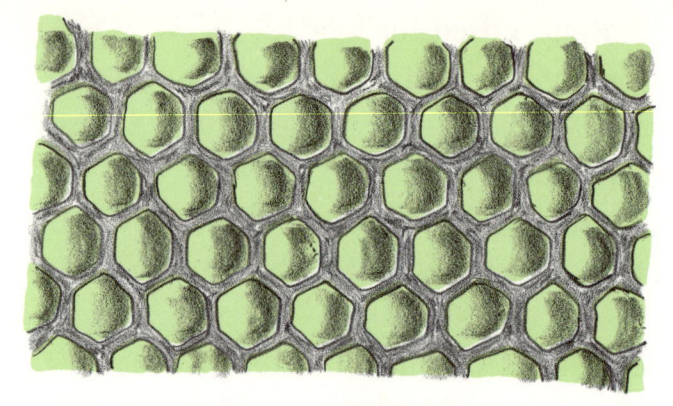

Cells in a honey comb

A honey bee   **A bee hive**

Honey, Wax, and Ink

Some insects help us when we *take* things from them. Other insects help us when we *make* things from them.

We take honey and wax from bees. Bees make honey and wax from the nectar they gather.

The wax forms in small scales on the underneath side of the bee's abdomen. The wax is used by the bees for making little six-sided rooms called *cells*. Many cells together make a *comb*. Eggs are laid in the cells.

The bee makes honey in its *honey sac*. Some of the nectar the bee swallows goes into the honey sac. Chemicals change the nectar into honey. Then the bee spits the honey up. It spits the honey into the cells of the comb. The honey is food for the larvae that hatch from the eggs.

Beekeepers fool the bees into making extra cells and filling them with honey, even though no eggs have been laid in these cells. Special machines remove the honey from these cells. This is the honey that the beekeepers sell.

They get beeswax by melting down old honeycombs. Beeswax makes a fine polish.

We make a very good writing ink with the help of a small wasp. These little wasps feed on oak trees in the western part of Asia, near the city of Aleppo. These wasps are gall insects. They make *Aleppo galls*.

A very fine black ink is made from Aleppo galls. Under the laws of Massachusetts, this ink must be used for writing all public records.

A cochineal insect

Insects for Varnish and Dye

Varnish is often used on wood instead of paint. Good varnish has *lac* in it. Lac is made from a scale insect that lives in the Far East.

Many lac insects live together on the twigs of trees. The female has a pointed beak. She sucks sap through her beak. Most of the sap passes out of her body. It forms a scale of lac on her back. Because the insects are crowded together on the twig, the scales come together to make a sheet. The insects keep feeding under this sheet of lac.

Lac-covered twigs are then cut from the trees. The scale and insects are separated from the wood by putting the twigs in hot water. Lac for varnish is made from the scale. Artists' colors called "lakes" are made from the dead insects.

Beautiful red dye is made from the *cochineal* (KOTCH-i-neel) insect, a scale insect found in Mexico. It lives on cactus plants. Its abdomen is dark red. Most cochineal insects are female. Dye is made from female insects that are filled with eggs. The female is very large then. It takes 70,000 insects to make a pound of dye.

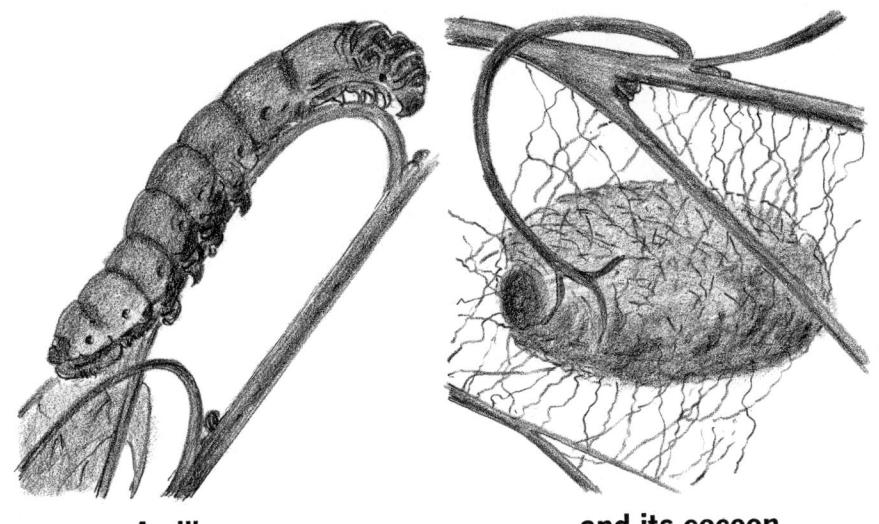

A silkworm...   **...and its cocoon**

A Cradle of Silk

There are caterpillars that make silk. The caterpillar spins a silk thread. It wraps the thread around itself many times to make a *cocoon* (kuh-KOON). The caterpillar spins about a half mile of thread to make its cocoon.

This caterpillar is called the *silkworm*. It is the larva of a large white moth. It eats the leaves of mulberry trees.

Silkgrowers gather the cocoons and heat them to kill the caterpillars inside. Then they unwind the silk of the cocoons and wind it on reels. Several strands of silk are twisted together to make thread for weaving and sewing.

It takes about 3,000 cocoons to make 1 pound of silk.

Silk is not used very much today. Man-made fibers like rayon and nylon have taken its place.

Most silk comes from China and Japan.

WORD LIST

Adult (a-DULT) — The full-grown insect.

Antennae (an-TEN-ee) — An insect's feelers. They look like stiff hairs. They are attached to the insect's head.

Anther (AN-ther) — The male part of a flower. It makes pollen.

Chrysalis (KRISS-a-liss) — What a caterpillar changes into. Later the chrysalis changes into an adult insect.

Cocoon (kuh-KOON) — The blanket of silk thread in which some caterpillars wrap themselves. It is the pupa of some insects.

Fertilize (FUR-till-ize) — In a flower, the joining of pollen and an egg cell to make a seed.

Larva (LAR-va) — It hatches from an insect's egg. A caterpillar is a larva.

Nectar (NECK-tar) — A sweet syrup made by some flowers. It is gathered by insects as food.

Ovary (O-va-ree) — The bottom part of the pistil. The egg cells are made in the ovary.

Pistil (PIS-till) — The female part of a flower.

Pollen (POLL-en) — A yellow dust made by the anther of a flower. It comes together with the egg cell of a flower to make a seed.

Pupa (PEW-pa) — Same as chrysalis.

Stigma (STIG-ma) — The top part of the pistil. It receives the pollen.